Earth's Rock Cycle

Nancy Kelly Allen

PowerKiDS press.

New York

For Collin

Published in 2009 by The Rosen Publishing Group, Inc.
29 East 21st Street, New York, NY 10010

First Edition

Editor: Amelie von Zumbusch
Book Design: Kate Laczynski
Photo Researcher: Jessica Gerweck

Photo Credits: Cover, pp. 1, 4, 6, 10, 12, 16, 18, 20 Shutterstock.com; p. 8 © G. Brad Lewis/ Getty Images; p. 14 © NASA/digital version by Science Faction/Getty Images.

Library of Congress Cataloging-in-Publication Data

Allen, Nancy Kelly, 1949–
  Earth's rock cycle / Nancy Kelly Allen. — 1st ed.
      p. cm. — (Rock it!)
  Includes index.
  ISBN 978-1-4358-2762-2 (library binding) — ISBN 978-1-4358-3185-8 (pbk.)
ISBN 978-1-4358-3191-9 (6-pack)
  1. Petrology—Juvenile literature. 2. Geochemical cycles—Juvenile literature. I. Title.
  QE432.2.A55 2009
  552—dc22
                                      2008035594

Manufactured in the United States of America

CONTENTS

THE ROCK CYCLE

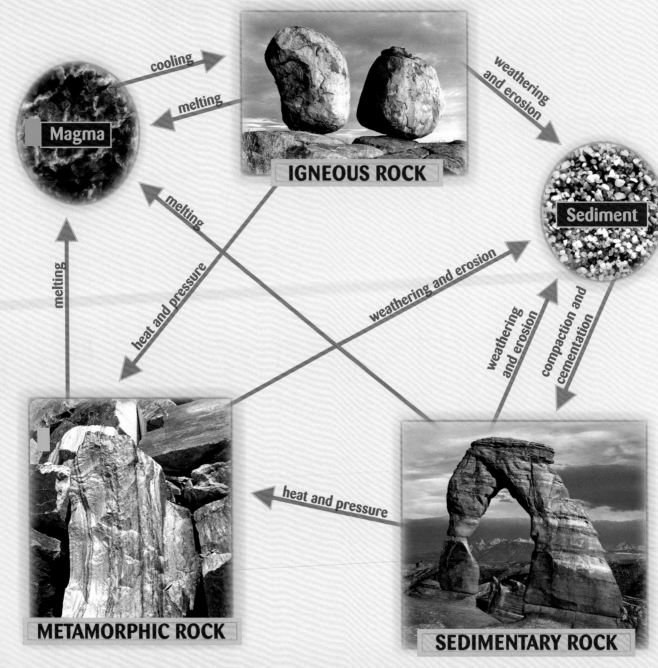

cooling

melting

Magma

weathering and erosion

IGNEOUS ROCK

Sediment

melting

melting

heat and pressure

weathering and erosion

weathering and erosion

compaction and cementation

heat and pressure

METAMORPHIC ROCK

SEDIMENTARY ROCK

No Beginning or End

Many people think of rocks as solid and never changing. However, Earth's rocks are always changing form. These changes are known as the rock **cycle**.

Scientists class Earth's rocks into three groups. These are igneous rocks, metamorphic rocks, and sedimentary rocks. Igneous rocks form when melted rock hardens. Sedimentary rocks are formed from little bits of matter, called sediment. This sediment is generally made up of tiny pieces of rock. Metamorphic rock is created when heat and **pressure** change the **minerals** in sedimentary rocks and igneous rocks.

Over time, any kind of rock can become any other kind of rock. The rock cycle has no beginning or end.

Under mountains, Earth's crust may be as much as 44 miles (70 km) thick. However, most of the crust under oceans is just 6 miles (10 km) thick.

Down to the Core

If you visited Earth's center, you would first pass through the rocks of the crust. The crust is made of plates that push together, move apart, and slide past each other. It is thinner under oceans and thicker under land. Under land, the crust is generally 20 to 30 miles (32–48 km) thick.

The second **layer**, the mantle, is about 1,800 miles (2,900 km) thick. It **contains** hot, melted rock. Below that lies the core. The **outer** core is 1,430 miles (2,300 km) thick and filled with melted metals. Deepest of all is the **inner** core, which is made of solid metals.

Your trip to the center of Earth would be almost 4,000 miles (6,440 km) long. It would also be very hot. The core is about 12,600° F (6,982° C)!

Kilauea, in Hawaii, is one of the world's most active volcanoes. It has been erupting, or spilling out lava, steadily since 1983.

Fire Fountains

Sometimes the plates in Earth's crust crash together. This pushes the edge of one of the plates under ground. It also produces so much heat that some rocks melt. Melted rock, called magma, gets trapped in pockets deep under ground. Over time, magma cools and forms igneous rocks. Most rocks in Earth's crust are igneous rocks.

Sometimes magma flows to Earth's **surface** before it cools and hardens. Lava, as magma on Earth's surface is called, escapes through breaks in Earth's crust, called volcanoes. Some volcanoes throw lava, **ash**, and steam into the air. Lava flows slowly out of other volcanoes.

Volcanoes in Hawaii sometimes shoot sprays of lava known as fire fountains. These fountains can rise hundreds of feet (m) into the air.

The igneous rock basalt sometimes forms
hexagonal, or six-sided, columns as it cools.
You can see columnar basalt at Iceland's
Skaftafell National Park.

From Hot to Cold

Red-hot magma forms two kinds of igneous rocks. Magma that cools inside Earth forms intrusive igneous rock. Magma that hardens only after it has flowed to Earth's surface and become known as lava forms extrusive igneous rocks.

Andesite and basalt are extrusive igneous rocks. Andesite is named for the Andes mountains, where the rock is common. Andesite forms from sticky lava. Igneous rocks that cool quickly, such as andesite and basalt, have small, smooth grains. Granite is a strong intrusive igneous rock. Granite cools slowly, so it has large grains.

Mount Rushmore, in South Dakota, is a giant rock monument. It has the heads of four American presidents cut in granite.

Waves crashing against the coast of Gozo, an island in the Mediterranean Sea, wear away the island's cliffs. This is one kind of weathering.

Falling Apart

Rocks on Earth's surface are always breaking apart. The breaking down of rocks into smaller pieces is called weathering. Weathering happens many ways. Sometimes water fills holes in rocks and then **freezes**. Ice spreads to fill more space than water does, so the ice presses against the rocks, and the rocks break.

Waves pound against rocks and move pieces of rock back and forth. Rock pieces become so small that they form sand. Rivers also break down rocks as water flows. Wind blows grains of sand against rocks. The blowing sand wears away rocks, little by little. Any rock that wind or water touches gets slowly worn down.

Glaciers, such as these ones in the Andes, are slow-moving masses of ice. Glaciers pull sediment along with them as they move.

A Washout

Water and wind also carry sediment, such as broken pieces of rocks, from one area to another. This action is called erosion. Erosion moves sediment across Earth's surface in several ways. Rain washes away bits of rock. Large ice blocks break from mountains and carry sediment. The wind blows small bits of sediment to new places.

In time, all sediment gets deposited, or dropped, somewhere. Streams and rivers deposit sediment at the bottoms of seas and lakes. Large rivers, such as the Mississippi River, deposit thousands of tons (t) of sediment every day.

Every day, erosion carries away rocks at Niagara Falls, a huge waterfall that lies between Canada and the United States. About 1 foot (.3 m) of rock is lost each year.

Antelope Canyon is made of sandstone. Weathering and erosion formed this canyon, or very narrow valley, on Navajo lands in Arizona.

16

A Wet Start

Many layers of sediment build up over time. Much sediment is rock, but dead plants and the shells of sea animals can become sediment, too. Each new layer of sediment buries the older layers deeper under ground and adds more weight. The weight of the layers forces the sediment near the bottom to bond together. This sediment hardens into sedimentary rock.

Sandstone is a sedimentary rock that often forms in areas that had water flowing through sand. Sediment made of sea animals that lived millions of years ago forms limestone rock. A sedimentary rock called oil shale forms when dead animals settle at the bottoms of lakes.

The metamorphic rock marble is often used
for buildings and monuments. The Trevi Fountain,
in Rome, Italy, has many marble statues.

Hot and Heavy

Metamorphic rocks form when the minerals in sedimentary or igneous rocks change. Pressure and heat cause these changes. The deeper rocks are buried inside Earth, the more the pressure and heat increase. When the pressure becomes great enough to fold or **squeeze** rocks, the minerals in those rocks change.

When heat reaches certain **temperatures**, the minerals in rocks start changing. The sedimentary rock shale becomes a metamorphic rock, slate, when the temperature reaches about 400° F (204° C). The metamorphic rock gneiss forms at 1,472° F (800° C). Most metamorphic rocks form underground, but hot lava flowing over sedimentary and igneous rocks can also form metamorphic rocks.

Many mountain ranges are still growing.
The Himalayas, seen here, grow .2 inch
(5 mm) taller each year.

New Life in Old Rock

We can see signs of the rock cycle taking place all around us. Have you ever felt dust in the wind? Dust settles to the ground and hardens into sedimentary rock. Though metamorphic rocks form deep under Earth, you can see them being pushed up in mountain ranges, such as the Alps and the Andes.

Volcanoes around the world make igneous rocks. If you dived to the bottom of the ocean, you would see places where magma flows through cracks in the seafloor and forms rock **ridges**. This action, called seafloor spreading, happens again and again. Seafloor spreading makes the Atlantic Ocean grow about 8 inches (20 cm) wider every year.

A Piece of the Action

Earth is a rocky planet filled with action. Volcanoes **erupt**. Mountain ranges, such as the Sierra Nevada, push up through Earth's crust. The rock cycle shows us how rocks take different forms and are always changing.

We all need rocks. Rocks provide blocks for buildings. Rocks contain iron and other minerals from which we make tools, too. Roads, glass, and monuments are all made with rocks. Scientists, called geologists, study the rock cycle to understand our planet. The better we understand Earth and the rocks that form it, the more uses for rocks we are likely to find. The good news is that Earth will never run out of rocks!

GLOSSARY

ash (ASH) Pieces of tiny rock that shoot out of a volcano when it blows.

contains (kun-TAYNZ) Holds.

cycle (SY-kul) Actions that happen in the same order over and over.

erupt (ih-RUPT) To break open.

freezes (FREEZ-ez) Makes something so cold it hardens.

inner (IN-nur) On the inside.

layer (LAY-er) One thickness of something.

minerals (MIN-rulz) Natural things that are not animals, plants, or other living things.

outer (OWT-ur) On the outside.

pressure (PREH-shur) A force that pushes on something.

ridges (RIJ-ez) Long, narrow chains of hills or mountains.

squeeze (SKWEEZ) To force together.

surface (SER-fes) The outside of anything.

temperatures (TEM-pur-cherz) How hot or cold things are.

INDEX

WEB SITES

Due to the changing nature of Internet links, PowerKids Press has developed an online list of Web sites related to the subject of this book. This site is updated regularly. Please use this link to access the list:
www.powerkidslinks.com/rockit/cycle/